GROUND ZERO SPIRIT

Written by Jeffrey Page

**Photographed by
The Record and Herald News**

presented by

North Jersey Media Group

The Record

Herald News

The photographers whose work is exhibited in this book include Thomas E. Franklin, James W. Anness, Mel Evans, Beth Balbierz, Danielle P. Richards, Carmine Galasso, Don Smith, Chris Pedota, Tariq Zehawi, and Adam Lisberg of *The Record*, and Ryan Mercer and Kevin R. Wexler of the *Herald News*. *Record* Columnist and Senior Writer Jeffrey Page is the book's author. *Record* Photo Director Rich Gigli selected the photographs for the book. The book is a project of the Specialty Publications Division of North Jersey Media Group.

Published by Pediment Publishing,
a division of The Pediment Group, Inc.
www.pediment.com
printed in Canada

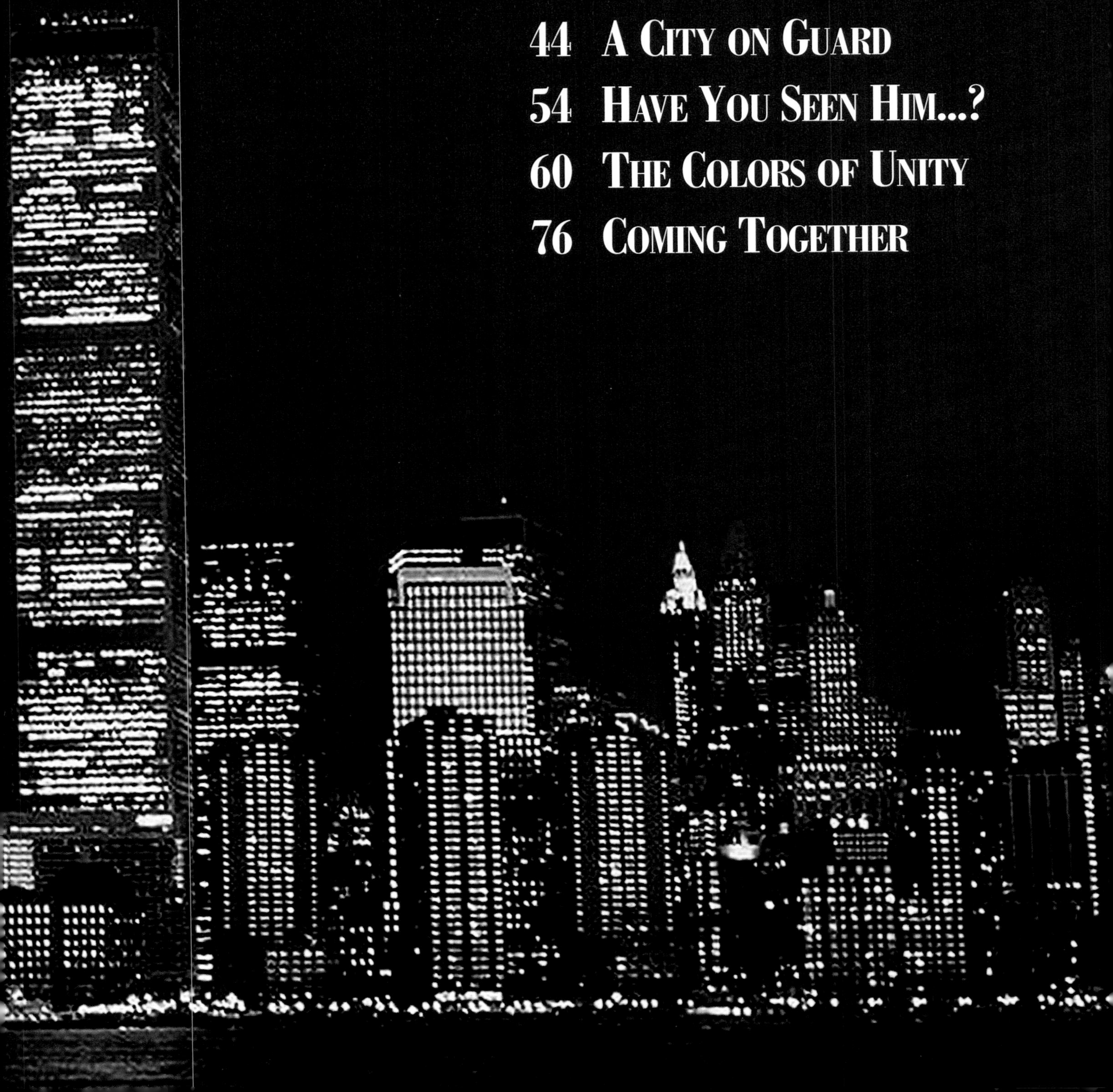

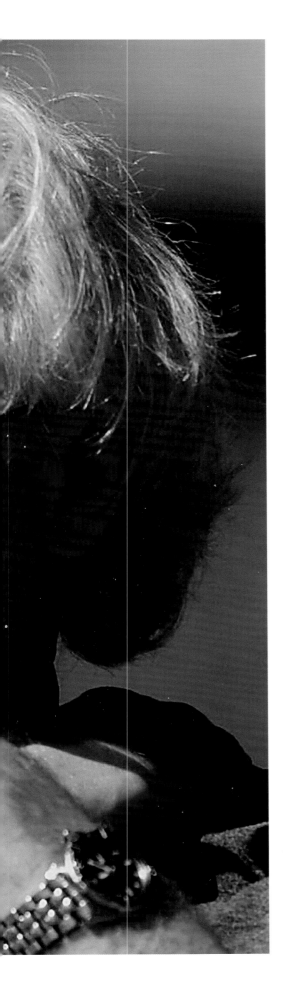

FOREWORD

The story that changed America began on just another Tuesday morning.

Reporters, photographers, and editors had just started drifting into The Record newsroom in Hackensack, N.J.

The writer of this book, Jeffrey Page, was on the phone talking with a friend about the health of the friend's wife. Suddenly, Charles Austin, the religion writer, slammed down his own phone and said with great alarm there had been some kind of plane crash at the World Trade Center.

Quickly, some people went to the newsroom windows, which afford a spectacular view of the New York skyline. Huge clouds of black smoke rose into the sky from the doomed North Tower.

Others hurried to the televisions. At first they just gazed at what seemed like a terrible accident. Then, before their unbelieving eyes, they saw another plane slam into the South Tower.

So much for accidents.

Editors grabbed for the phones to call their writers. Assignments were yelled across the room. Reporters and photographers dashed out of the building to their cars and the adrenaline-fueled drive east and south toward the World Trade Center.

By early afternoon, an Extra edition was running on the press. It was The Record's first Extra since the assassination of President John F. Kennedy in 1963.

TERROR HITS HOME, the Page 1 headline screamed.

The picture showed huge billows of smoke and flame roiling out of the World Trade Center.

The lead paragraph on the Page 1 story said it all: "Terrorism unprecedented in American history — the dive-bombing and flaming collapse of the World Trade Center, explosions at the Pentagon, and the hijacking and crash of a commercial jet after takeoff from Newark — claimed untold lives today, plunging the nation into panic and sending U.S. authorities on alert for wide catastrophe."

It was Sept. 11.

This book is the story of the first two weeks of the new America.

It documents the work of photographers from The Record and the Herald News during those two weeks. It chronicles what they witnessed. It documents pieces of life in northern New Jersey, and it forms a historical record of this devastating time. It is dedicated to the firefighters, emergency workers, police personnel, and medical caregivers who worked so valiantly at the scene and in the following days, and to the victims of the attack and their families. Proceeds from this book will be donated to the North Jersey Media Group Disaster Relief Fund.

For information about the fund, visit www.GroundZeroSpirit.org.

Previous page: (AP/Mark Lennihan)

Left: **A couple at Sinatra Park on the banks of the Hudson River in Hoboken, N.J., after both towers of the trade center collapsed.** (Kevin Wexler)

> " *I was horrified and angered on different levels. I'm a New Yorker. I was watching my city be bombed by terrorists. I felt we were let down by our intelligence. On a personal level, I had two cousins unaccounted for and didn't realize they were OK until the next day.* "

– Carmine Galasso, staff photographer,
The Record (Bergen County, N.J.)

> " *It was the worst professional, saddest and most tragic day of my life. A collective lead blanket of sadness surrounded everything. Going to Ground Zero was numbing. It was surreal in a monochromatic way. I'm used to Manhattan being colorful, with yellow cabs and flashy signs. It was as if the color was taken out of our images.* "

– James W. Anness, staff photographer,
The Record (Bergen County, N.J.)

> " *I thought a pilot of a private plane suffered a heart attack and crashed into the World Trade Center. I never thought of a deliberate act. As I was making my way down to the ferry terminal to try to get to the scene, I heard about a second plane hitting the other tower. That thought was just too hard to believe, and I switched radio stations thinking it was a mistake. Then I saw the skyline...*
>
> *The most poignant image I remember is from the next day, a pedestrian bridge facing the smoldering remains of the towers. Someone had written "God Bless" in the dust and ash on the railing of the bridge. I think that's when everything started to sink in for me. I can only hope that we emerge stronger and braver as a result of all this, and that those who died didn't do so in vain.* "

– Danielle Richards, staff photographer,
The Record (Bergen County, N.J.)

> " *I got caught in the blast of dust 2-3 blocks from Ground Zero. It swallowed you up, everything went deathly quiet and completely black. For 60 seconds I had no idea how I was going to get out. Then I took a lens cleaning cloth covered with a polymer to breathe through. I found another man in a similar situation, we walked out together, and I brought him to an ambulance. After I calmed down, I went back in to get my job done.* "

– Ryan Mercer, chief photographer,
Herald News (Passaic County, N.J.)

> " *I have never been fully aware of the power of photography until I made this photograph of three New York City firemen raising the U.S. flag atop the rubble that was the World Trade Center. I have received literally thousands of phone calls and hundreds of e-mails, mostly from strangers. From around the world people have told me how this photograph has touched them, and that has touched me. Some have told me about their lost loved ones, others about how they escaped certain death. Others just wanted to tell me how this one photograph gave them hope and optimism in the wake of this horrible tragedy. Although it has been hard for me to separate myself and my sudden notoriety from this picture, it has given me some comfort to know that in some small way I may have helped Americans get through this tragedy. And I am hoping that with the sales of this photo, we can help raise money for victims of this disaster. And that also speaks to me about the immense power of photojournalism. Peace.* "

– Thomas E. Franklin, staff photographer,
The Record (Bergen County, N.J.)

" It was eerie for it to be
empty. I never saw it
empty before. It was
like a ghost town. "

– Mel Evans, staff photographer,
The Record (Bergen County, N.J.)

" I saw the second tower get hit as I was driving to work on the Turnpike.
By the time I got off Exit 13A, the second tower came down. I looked
around and it was gone. I never thought they would fall down.

The lines for the telephone were 20-25 people deep. No one could get enough information fast enough about what was going on. People congregated around
a Channel 2 news van (on site to cover the news) to get information. "

– Beth Balbierz, staff photographer,
The Record (Bergen County, N.J.)

" One of my assignments on the day of the massacre was to get photos of people who lined up out the door at a local blood bank to
give blood. They all wanted to do something to help the victims. I was
impressed. The people were young and old, male and female, black, white,
beige, and every other shade, and they all had one thing in com-
mon. Today they were Americans. No hyphens. Just Americans. "

– Don Smith, staff photographer,
The Record (Bergen County, N.J.)

" When I woke up on the morning of Sept. 11, I turned on the television
like most mornings, not knowing that what I would see would change the
way I see the world as a photojournalist. I feel that we are more than photographers, we are also documenting our history today, and some of these images will be
used in future history books. These books will not just show the tragedy
but also how Americans have come together to comfort one another. "

– Tariq Zehawi, staff photographer,
The Record (Bergen County, N.J.)

" As I took pictures from Hoboken, I realized that I had never seen such a large group of
strangers who knew exactly what each other was thinking without saying a word. People
were looking up to the sky where two planes flew into our tallest buildings. Now all they could see
was a dark gray cloud of smoke. Soon they would bow their heads or look away when they could not
stand the sight anymore. Everyone with cameras began to take pictures not only of the horrific plume
of smoke, which looked like a war zone even from across the Hudson, but of the Empire State
Building, which everyone thought could be the next skyscraper falling to the ground. "

– Kevin Wexler, staff photographer,
Herald News (Passaic County, N.J.)

" It was obvious this would touch everyone. I had to cover funerals and memori-
al services for people I never met but felt terrible sorrow for. I later found that I
went to high school with three New York firefighters who died at the WTC. It was impos-
sible to emotionally detach. The worst as well as ironic moment was going downtown
and seeing the rubble that was the WTC, realizing these two incredible and
complex structures were brought down by people who live and hide in caves. "

– Chris Pedota, staff photographer,
The Record (Bergen County, N.J.)

THE ATTACK

It was still summer, the carefree time.

In the Financial District just before 9 a.m., thousands of people climbed out of the subway and PATH tubes to make their way to work at the World Trade Center. Thousands of others were already at their desks. It was a thoroughly unextraordinary Tuesday morning.

Then the hijacked planes arrived high over Manhattan.

Where were you at 8:50 a.m. on Sept. 11, 2001?

Sept. 11 was one of the days in the life of America we'll remember forever. Always in the years and decades to come, we'll be able to say precisely what we were doing at 8:50 a.m., where we were, whom we were with. The Sept. 11 attacks have taken their place with other events on other dark days that transformed us and our nation, days whose minutest details we will always hold fast in memory: Pearl Harbor, the assassinations of President John F. Kennedy and Martin Luther King, the resignation of President Richard Nixon, even the death of JFK Jr.

Television and radio stations broke into their programming to report that an airplane had struck the World Trade Center. If you were near a window, you hurried to it. The sight was unbelievable; enormous surges of black smoke rising from the upper floors of the North Tower.

Maybe you were among the people who thought it was a horrible accident. But if you rushed back to the television set, maybe you

Previous page: **Before the start of a new age in America, the World Trade Center towers define the Lower Manhattan skyline. But on Sept. 11, 2001 – another date that will live in infamy – the twin towers were erased in a devastating and unthinkable act of terrorism.** (AP/Ed Bailey)

Above: **Any thought that the crash of a jet carrying 92 people into the North Tower was a horrible accident is dashed 13 minutes later when a second plane, carrying 65 people, flies at full throttle into the South Tower of the trade center.** (AP/Carmen Taylor)

Right: **An unimaginable sight moments after the second plane hits: One of the 110-story towers spews clouds of black, acrid smoke in the morning sky while the second tower explodes in a gargantuan ball of fire.** (AP/Kelley Sane)

Opposite: **With the explosion, tons of debris – steel, glass, office furniture – burst free and rain down on the street.** (AP/Chao Soi Cheong)

saw the second plane fly into the South Tower and then you knew the truth. You didn't need some talking head to explain it.

Maybe you stood transfixed, stunned, not understanding, yet somehow understanding perfectly that this was no mishap and that the city, the nation, the world — and you — had just changed in a way no one could have imagined on Sept. 10.

The first day of America's future was only just beginning.

At 9:30 a.m., a commercial airliner crashed into the Pentagon. Then 1 World Trade Center collapsed. At 10 a.m., a passenger flight crashed in a field in Pennsylvania, and 30 minutes later, 2 World Trade Center fell in on itself.

President George W. Bush told the nation the conspiracy was the work of terrorists who had hijacked the four planes, and that the deaths of Americans would be avenged. Officials quickly placed the blame on Osama bin Laden, an angry Saudi banished by the Saudi Arabian government and living under the protection of the Taliban regime of Afghanistan.

The Taliban could surrender Bin Laden or face the consequences, the President said. And then, he advised the world's nations that — in what he described as a war on terrorism and countries that allow it to flourish — they either were with the United States or against the United States.

War on the Taliban and Bin Laden's al-Qaeda terrorist forces began Oct. 7 when United States and British planes attacked targets throughout Afghanistan. The air war began just two days after an employee of a supermarket tabloid based in Boca Raton, Fla., died of anthrax. It was just the start of anthrax scares in various parts of the country. Were they part of the Bin Laden conspiracy? Or were they the work of home-grown terrorists? No one knew.

As late as the end of October, the extent of the domestic devastation was incalculable.

In the ruins of the World Trade Center were 4,569 missing people. Recovered were 458 bodies (all but 40 identified.) At the Pentagon, 125 people had been killed, and 265 people had been killed on the four hijacked planes.

All this in the catastrophe of Sept. 11, a time that seems like a hundred years ago, and yet at times seems like 20 minutes ago.

Left: The South Tower is gone. The fires in the highest stories of the North Tower continue to rage. (Danielle Richards)

Below: The view of the last minutes of the North Tower from Exchange Place in Jersey City. In New York's downtown streets, the smoke is so thick, it turns the morning into a dark, grim entrance to hell. (Thomas Franklin)

Opposite: The view from uptown, just north of the Empire State Building, which had been the tallest skyscraper in New York before the trade center was built and which, in another 100 minutes, would again be the highest as the South and North Towers drop to earth. (AP/Patrick Sison)

Right: What panic looks like. People in the street run – as they have never run in their lives – from the incredible scene of the South Tower's fall. (AP/Suzanne Plunkett)

Above: **The immediate task for thousands of people was to get away. One way out of lower Manhattan was the Brooklyn Bridge, whose pedestrian walkway was the path to safety.**
(AP/Daniel Shanken)

Right: **The view from Hamilton Park in Weehawken, N.J.**
(Danielle Richards)

Above: With both towers gone, some of the buildings they dwarfed for 30 years seem to rise. The tall structure at the extreme left is the Woolworth Building, which when it opened in 1913 was the tallest at 55 stories. It would be supplanted by the Chrysler Building, the Empire State Building, and finally by the World Trade Center. At right are three buildings of the World Financial Center, the headquarters of American Express in the building with the pyramid roof, and Merrill Lynch headquarters in the other two. (James Anness)

Left: It's not often you literally must run for your life. But how do you escape the falling trade center on crutches? A woman discovers her Galahad on Warren Street. He picks her up, crutches and all, and starts loping north.
(Ryan Mercer)

Above: **Hours after the terrorist attack, a man takes in the hugeness of the loss from Liberty State Park in Jersey City.** (James Anness)

Others: **Shrouded by choking smoke near West Street, firefighters encounter three slabs of latticed ironwork standing at precarious angles, the only things left standing of what had been symbols of New York.** (Right photo: Adam Lisberg, opposite top: Carmine Galasso, opposite bottom: Danielle Richards, opposite right: Ryan Mercer)

Previous page: **Late on Sept. 11, with hundreds of their colleagues unaccounted for, police, firefighters, rescue workers, and construction workers converge in the ruins.** (James Anness)

Right: **The fires continued to burn for weeks.** (Thomas Franklin)

Below: **Close examination sometimes means getting on your hands and knees.** (Adam Lisberg)

Left: Fallen beams create an eerie and treacherous landscape for firefighters searching for survivors.
(Thomas Franklin)

Below: Estimates were that more than 1 million tons of debris would have to be cleared from the World Trade Center site. Cars, trucks, and fire engines were pushed aside by raining wreckage as easily as a feather caught in a breeze.
(Thomas Franklin)

Right: **A section of the trade center remained standing days after the attack, taking the shape of a ghostly ship sailing off into the distance.** (Carmine Galasso)

Below: **How do you measure the extent of debris? Here, it's halfway up the tires of a wrecked New York Presbyterian Hospital Ambulance at Ground Zero.** (Thomas Franklin)

A passer-by takes in the stark contrast of devastation, street plants, and an untouched building.
(Beth Balbierz)

Top: **Life amid the ruins. Birds soar over Ground Zero.**
(Chris Pedota)

Right: **No television image could satisfactorily put Ground Zero into perspective. Here the wreckage dwarfs two firefighters.**
(Carmine Galasso)

Opposite: **Tons of rubble await examination by police and federal agents looking for evidence before it is carted to a landfill on Staten Island, where it will be checked again.**
(Carmine Galasso)

Firefighters taking a break from a job that seems endless.
(James Anness)

Right: **Two objects in the eye of the storm: A ruined ladder truck and a soldier who has seen enough for a while.**
(Mel Evans)

Below: **Searching for signs of survivors in a forest of steel beams that snapped like twigs.**
(Ryan Mercer)

Above: **National Guard troops taking up positions near Ground Zero.**
(Mel Evans)

Left: **Firefighters amid fallen iron.**
(Ryan Mercer)

Left and below: **The enormity of the loss of colleagues.** (Ryan Mercer, Thomas Franklin)

Bottom right: **Troops on patrol passing ruined firetrucks.** (Danielle Richards)

Right: **A study in gray as a police officer receives first aid.**
(Ryan Mercer)

Below: **The Comfort, a Navy hospital ship, housed 2,250 rescue workers in its two-week stay in New York. It served 17,000 meals and washed 4,400 pounds of laundry, and then returned to its home port of Baltimore.** (Norm Sutaria)

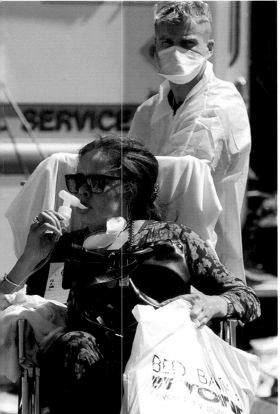

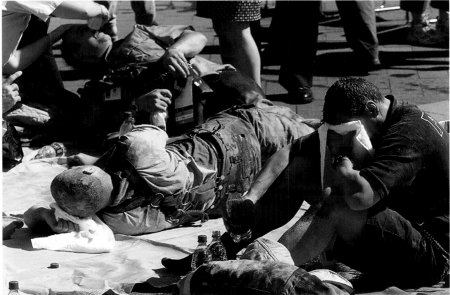

Many of the injured rescue workers and civilians were ferried across the Hudson to Jersey City where they received emergency treatment at Liberty State Park. Others were treated at the PATH station in Hoboken, N.J. (Thomas Franklin, Thomas Franklin, James Anness)

The image of Sept. 11. Three firemen from Brooklyn, George Johnson, Dan McWilliams, and Billy Eisengrein, run up the colors on a mast in the devastation of the World Trade Center. McWilliams took the flag from a yacht moored near the World Financial Center, and he and his two buddies raised it, giving a cheerless New York something to cheer about for decades to come.
(Thomas Franklin)

Did it really happen or was it a nightmare? Sept. 12 gave proof, at dawn, that the skyline, and by extension the American heart, had huge empty spaces. (Beth Balbierz)

Today's Agenda

- M&A Philosophy & Overview
- Citigroup M&A Activity
- M&A Execution
- Deal Review Process
- M&A Strategy Process
- Deal Execution
- Appendix I

THE DESPAIR

Everybody who has spent time at Ground Zero agrees that no televised image could portray its vastness, no written words could define its insanity, and certainly no spoken description could capture the horror of what the people in the World Trade Center experienced when the buildings fell.

There are no lenses wide enough, no words stark enough, no voice emotional enough to show you that which only your own eyes, ears, and nose can understand.

Day after day, people took a look at the mountain of devastation and, as is so characteristic of the human animal, clamped their hands over their mouths — not their eyes —when they saw the enormity of the New York tragedy.

Throughout the first two weeks after Sept. 11, Downtown Manhattan was a vision of despair. After all, how much destruction can you look at before the magnitude reaches your soul and wrenches your gut? How many times can you look at the ravages and understand that which can't be understood — that the overwhelming majority of the dead will never be found — before you have to take a walk over to a quiet place, rest your head in your hands, and allow yourself to grieve for people you never knew?

So members of a grateful populace pay their visits to the ruins, leave flowers, bring dry socks for the recovery workers and emergency service workers, clap cops on the back, shake hands with firefighters, cheer, and then go home.

After the steel and glass and plastic, the desks and chairs and file cabinets, the airplane parts and elevators and coffee pots plummeted to earth, it was paper, the stuff of business, that floated to the street. The agenda at Citigroup on the day of the attack had been mergers and acquisitions – a philosophical overview, the strategy, and the all-important execution of the deal. (Danielle Richards)

People use their hands to prevent themselves from speaking in times of trouble. (Clockwise from below). The Mayor of America, Rudolph Giuliani, seemed to be everywhere to comfort, to mourn, to encourage, to reassure, to hearten, and to inspire a constituency that stretched out from the Five Boroughs; a woman at Liberty Street; a woman resting on a curb near Ground Zero; Kari Sherman, who had just arrived from London, praying for friends who worked at the World Trade Center; a woman waiting for her sister to arrive on the ferry to Weehawken; Lawrence Jones of Jersey City waiting for his wife, Janene, who worked at the trade center and who survived, Aziza Musleh, Nancy Fayed, and Rubbayyia Salaam, students at Al-Ghazaly High School in Teaneck, N.J. (Photos on this page by Beth Balbierz; photos on opposite page, clockwise from top right by Beth Balbierz, Danielle Richards, Danielle Richards, Danielle Richards, and Thomas Franklin)

Downtown the smoke and dust remained intense long after the attacks of Sept. 11. A young girl uses a disposable mask. A woman protects herself with a blouse while a man breathes through a hand towel.
(Photos at left by Danielle Richards; photo above by Mel Evans)

Below: Even as they waited on line at the Bergen County Blood Center in Paramus, N.J., donors seemed lost in private thoughts about life and death, about peace and war, about Sept. 11 and the days before and after. Christine Soliman, wearing stethoscope, takes medical information from a donor, Tom Pellegrino. (Don Smith)

Left: In the days after the attack, people going to their jobs in the Financial District left flowers and fliers about peace vigils, for cops, firemen, emergency services workers, and members of the National Guard. (Chris Pedota)

Below: He was commissioned by the Firefighters Association of Missouri and made at a Matthews International Corp. foundry in Parma, Italy. On Sept. 11, he had not yet cleared customs at Kennedy Airport. Then the World Trade Center was attacked and JFK was closed. The president of Matthews contacted the Missouri firefighters and suggested they donate him to the NYFD. Missouri agreed and for now at least, this 2,700-pound bronze sculpture of a fireman at prayer rests at 44th Street and Eighth Avenue, where more than a few people have placed candles in tribute. (Tariq Zehawi)

Right: **At a news conference in which members of the NYPD's Emergency Services Unit discussed their experiences at Ground Zero, Police Officer Stephen Stefanakos comforts a comrade, Glen Klein.**
(Beth Balbierz)

Below: **The enormity of the death and devastation was too much even for some professionals. One emergency medical technician comforts another when the horror builds to dangerous levels.**
(Carmine Galasso)

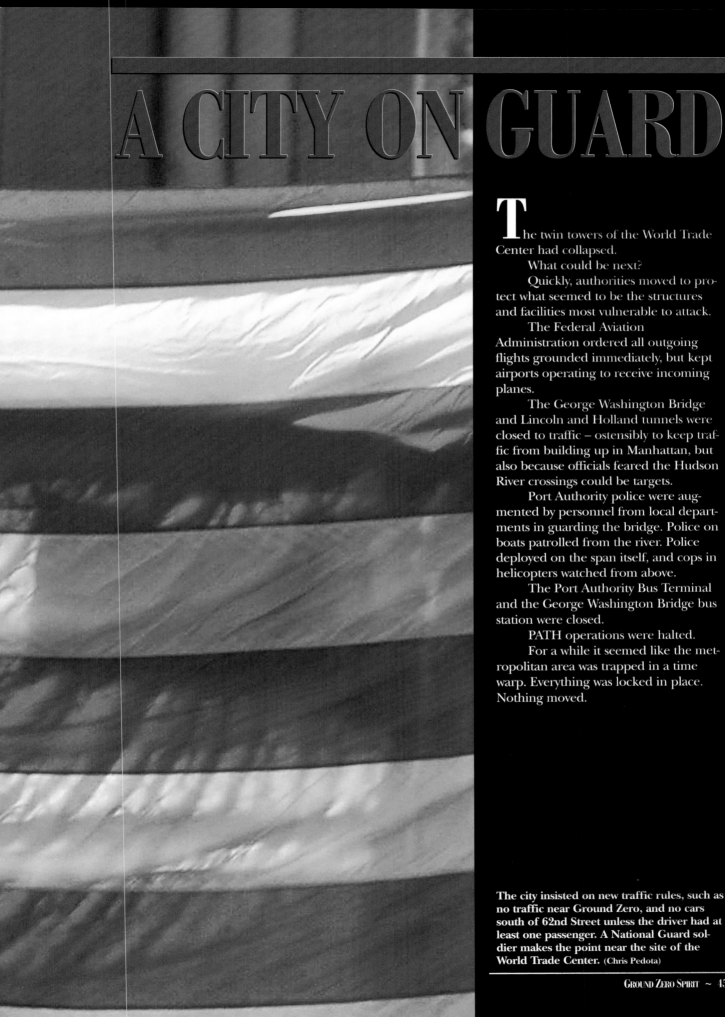

A CITY ON GUARD

The twin towers of the World Trade Center had collapsed.

What could be next?

Quickly, authorities moved to protect what seemed to be the structures and facilities most vulnerable to attack.

The Federal Aviation Administration ordered all outgoing flights grounded immediately, but kept airports operating to receive incoming planes.

The George Washington Bridge and Lincoln and Holland tunnels were closed to traffic – ostensibly to keep traffic from building up in Manhattan, but also because officials feared the Hudson River crossings could be targets.

Port Authority police were augmented by personnel from local departments in guarding the bridge. Police on boats patrolled from the river. Police deployed on the span itself, and cops in helicopters watched from above.

The Port Authority Bus Terminal and the George Washington Bridge bus station were closed.

PATH operations were halted.

For a while it seemed like the metropolitan area was trapped in a time warp. Everything was locked in place. Nothing moved.

The city insisted on new traffic rules, such as no traffic near Ground Zero, and no cars south of 62nd Street unless the driver had at least one passenger. A National Guard soldier makes the point near the site of the World Trade Center. (Chris Pedota)

Soon after the attack on the World Trade Center, authorities acted to guard other susceptible sites, such as the George Washington Bridge, which was closed to all traffic. Even the fence that provides access to the pedestrian path on the upper level was locked. In fact, the bridge likely hadn't been as devoid of traffic since 20 minutes before it opened in 1931. The Bergen County Police and Bergen County Sheriff's Department assisted the Port Authority Police, which monitored comings and goings at the bridge from the Palisades, the Hudson River, and from helicopters.

(Photos at opposite top and at left by Mel Evans; photo above by Don Smith; photo on following page by Carmine Galasso)

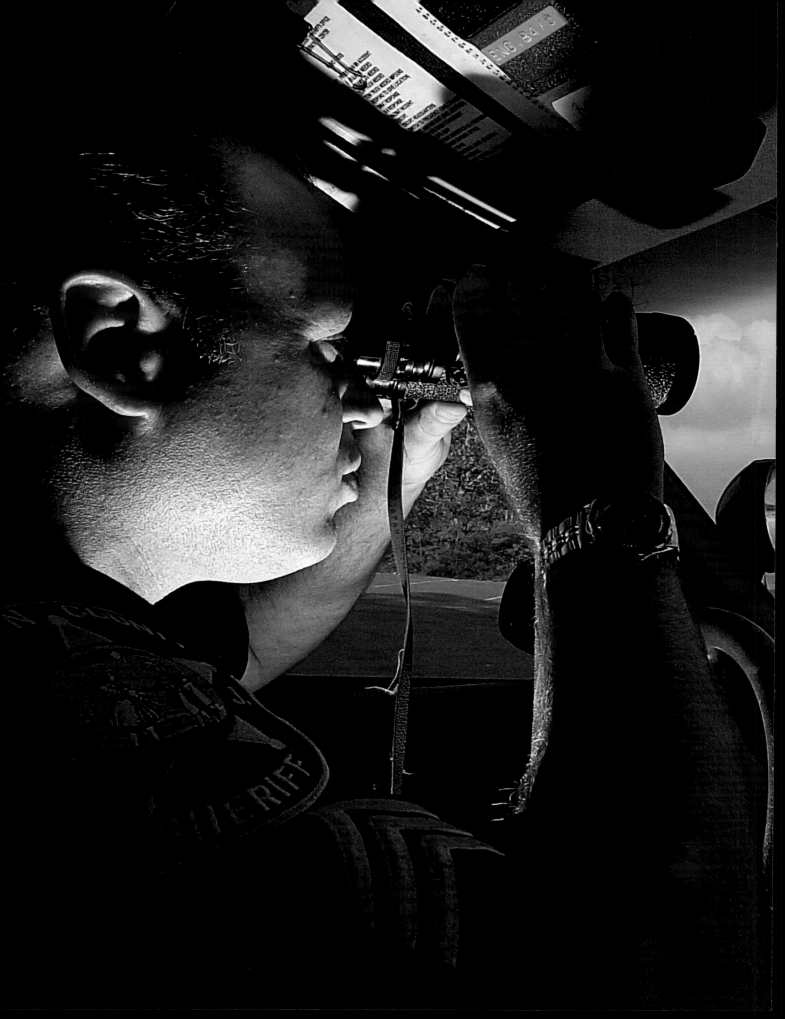

Newark International Airport was closed to incoming traffic and flights. In the movies you have seen police with rifles and shotguns at airports, not in America. Now the police were on guard and heavily armed, like Port Authority Police Officer Edmund Jackson. Once the airport was secured, people awaiting flights or incoming visitors were ordered out of the terminals. A mass of humanity streamed out of Terminal C. Even several days after the attack on the World Trade Center, airport operations were subject to disruption. Waiting on one row of seats were Priya Vasudev of Flemington, N.J., trying to return to medical school in Los Angeles and her parents, Dev and Immy Vasudev, seeing her off, and Rich Coyne awaiting the arrival of his friend from Orlando, Fla. (Photos at left and below by Beth Balbierz; bottom photo by Danielle Richards)

Traffic was worse than ever. A 30-minute delay in the approach to the Lincoln Tunnel is not unusual. In the days after the attack, the wait on Route 495, around the approach helix, past the tollbooths, and into the tubes was as long as two hours as the Holland Tunnel, connecting New Jersey and Downtown Manhattan, remained closed.

(James Anness)

At Ground Zero, the smoke, the dust, the asbestos, and the stench were getting worse, so the police used their gas masks, which may have made breathing a little easier, but apparently didn't do much to protect their eyes and ears. (Beth Balbierz)

"HAVE YOU SEEN HIM...?"

With the missing of the World Trade Center numbering in the thousands, the families' uncertainty became its own form of terror. The parents and spouses, children and friends of the missing converged at downtown help centers to check the lists of the dead and injured.

If they couldn't find the names of their loved ones, it meant — maybe — that a missing friend or relative was not buried in the rubble, but somehow managed to escape the buildings, was injured, and walked off in a daze to seek medical attention.

This was a long reach, but at a time of fearsome doubt, they had to grasp at anything that offered hope.

Those waiting for word took to the streets with posters, not unlike the ones you see on a post office bulletin board, though the people being sought weren't criminals. They were just ordinary people about to start an ordinary day's work at a moment when the life of the world came to an abrupt change.

They fastened their fliers on lampposts, on telephone booths, on traffic signal stanchions, on building walls, on any surface that would accept adhesive tape. They traveled from help center to hospital, from hospital to help center.

Nothing.

Have you seen my brother, they would ask.

No one had.

Please show this, they would implore the television camera operators and the newspaper photographers.

Pictures were snapped, TV cameras whirred.

It was wrenching work.

Previous page: **The man on the poster taped to the Wall of Remembrance at Liberty State Park is the missing Andrew LaCorte of Jersey City, the cousin of the woman on the left and brother of the woman on the right. Messages of support from strangers appear on the wall.** (Danielle Richards)

Right: **Among the missing, Mark Zangrilli of Pompton Plains, N.J., who called his family after the first plane hit the World Trade Center to say he was all right, and was not heard from again. Waiting to place his picture on the Wall of Remembrance is his sister, Linda Zangrilli Spinella of Wayne, N.J.** (Danielle Richards)

Above: **A block from the 69th Regiment Armory on Lexington Avenue, Claudia Sanchez of Englewood attaches a flier about her brother Alejandro Castano who was delivering office supplies to the South Tower when it collapsed.** (Tariq Zehawi)

Left: **Three women show pictures of their missing relative to passers-by on Lexington Avenue.** (Tariq Zehawi)

Right: **At Ground Zero, the grim work of recovery continues. Masked workers haul a body bag from the ruins.** (Ryan Mercer)

Left: Two dentists, Nicholas DeRobertis, left, and John Chibbaro, right, went to Ground Zero soon after the disaster to volunteer their assistance. The night of Sept. 11, they came across a knapsack owned by Ralph Bijou of Brooklyn in the rubble. They assumed he was buried. They dug. In fact, they dug all through the night but found nothing. Then, wishing to return the contents of his knapsack – a prayer book, a dark-colored clip-on tie, some paramedic training books, and some identity tags – to Bijou's family, they gave his name to a radio station. Bijou's mother heard the broadcast and called the dentists to say her son was all right. An emotional meeting took place several days later at Chibbaro's office in Westwood, N.J. "I am thankful I'm alive, and this has renewed my faith in man and God," Bijou said, gesturing toward DeRobertis and Chibbaro. (James Anness)

Below: Waiting outside Bellevue Hospital for even a shred of news about the missing. (Danielle Richards)

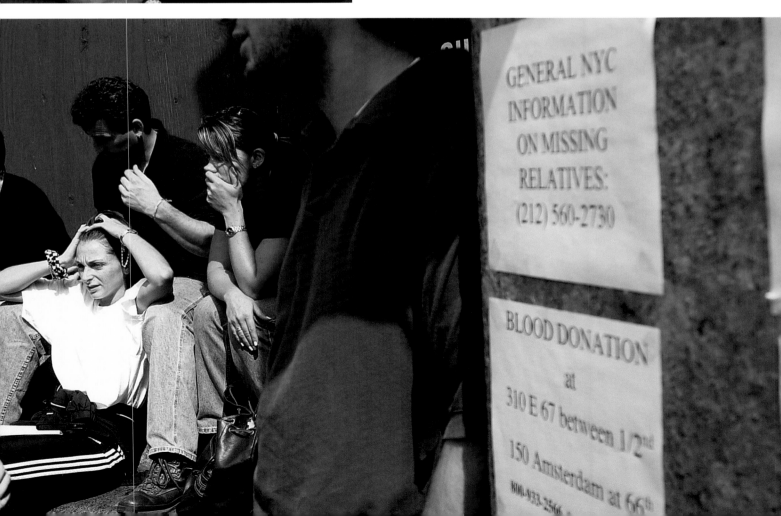

After a Port Authority crew unfurled the huge 90- by 60-foot flag from the superstructure of the George Washington Bridge, they waved smaller ones and motioned for motorists to honk for America. Drivers got the message. (Mel Evans)

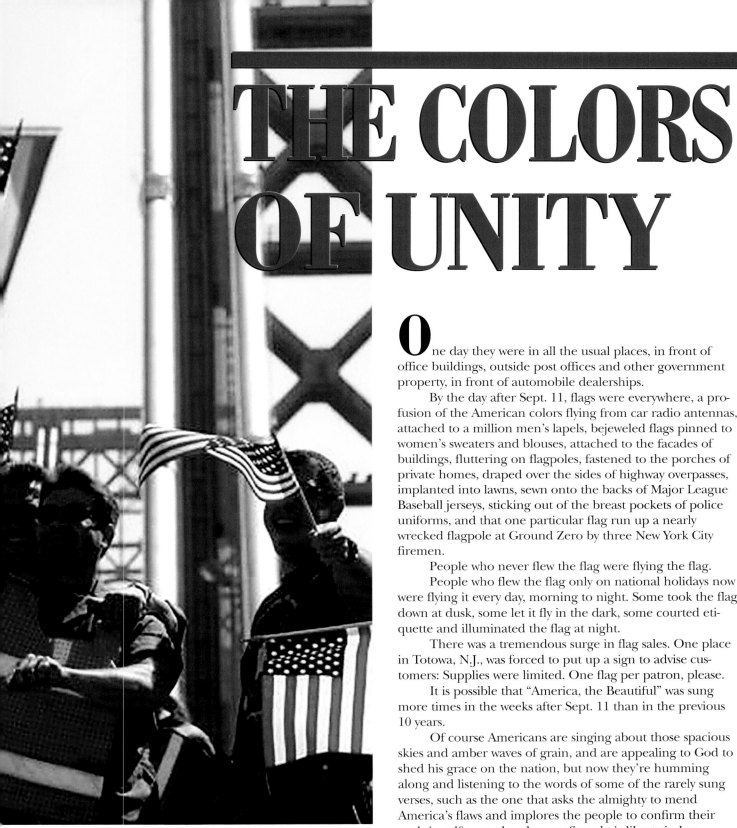

THE COLORS OF UNITY

One day they were in all the usual places, in front of office buildings, outside post offices and other government property, in front of automobile dealerships.

By the day after Sept. 11, flags were everywhere, a profusion of the American colors flying from car radio antennas, attached to a million men's lapels, bejeweled flags pinned to women's sweaters and blouses, attached to the facades of buildings, fluttering on flagpoles, fastened to the porches of private homes, draped over the sides of highway overpasses, implanted into lawns, sewn onto the backs of Major League Baseball jerseys, sticking out of the breast pockets of police uniforms, and that one particular flag run up a nearly wrecked flagpole at Ground Zero by three New York City firemen.

People who never flew the flag were flying the flag.

People who flew the flag only on national holidays now were flying it every day, morning to night. Some took the flag down at dusk, some let it fly in the dark, some courted etiquette and illuminated the flag at night.

There was a tremendous surge in flag sales. One place in Totowa, N.J., was forced to put up a sign to advise customers: Supplies were limited. One flag per patron, please.

It is possible that "America, the Beautiful" was sung more times in the weeks after Sept. 11 than in the previous 10 years.

Of course Americans are singing about those spacious skies and amber waves of grain, and are appealing to God to shed his grace on the nation, but now they're humming along and listening to the words of some of the rarely sung verses, such as the one that asks the almighty to mend America's flaws and implores the people to confirm their souls in self-control and to confirm their liberty in law.

And it may have been only since Sept. 11 that anyone heard some of the obscure verses of "America," such as: "Let music swell the breeze,/And ring from all the trees/Sweet freedom's song./Let mortal tongues awake,/Let all that breathe partake,/Let rocks their silence break,/The sound prolong."

Michael Greene, a construction worker who walked down the
West Side Highway to Ground Zero to volunteer, brought what
he thought he needed - his pack, his hard hat, and his flag.
(Danielle Richards)

Opposite: **With the World Trade Center gone, flags just across the Hudson River at Liberty State Park fly at half-staff.**
(Beth Balbierz)

Above: **Instead of planting bulbs, Frank Vopasek of Little Ferry, N.J., plants several score of flags on his lawn.**
(Mel Evans)

Left: **A priest says a blessing for the 400 participants in a march and candlelight vigil through the New Jersey cities of West New York and Union City.** (Tariq Zehawi)

Above: **One week after the attack, soldiers deploy near Bowling Green and Wall Street on the first day of resumed trading on the New York Stock Exchange.**
(Ryan Mercer)

Right: **Stock exchange employees returning to work.**
(Carmine Galasso)

Opposite: Louie Owens was so moved by the terrorist attack that he gave his house on Webster Avenue in Paterson, N.J., a whole new look and even found an appropriate shirt. (Danielle Richards)

Left: Shades of "Easy Rider:" Mark Yevchak of West Milford, N.J., tools along on his Harley-Davidson. (Mel Evans)

Below: On Main Street in Hackensack, N.J., a furniture store owner decided on new decor. (Mel Evans)

Opposite: **A National Guardsman on patrol near Duane Street, near Ground Zero.** (Carmine Galasso)

Left: **With no breeze to disturb them, flags fly at half-staff at Liberty State Park.** (Danielle Richards)

Below: **An emotional Barbara Ridgeway, a kindergarten teacher at the Washington Park School in Totowa, N.J., as red, white, and blue balloons are released. With her is one of her students, Dante Guarneri.** (Danielle Richards)

Right: **Message on a dust-covered window one week after the attack.** (Beth Balbierz)

Below: **Someone left a message in the dust along a pedestrian walkway over the West Side Highway a few blocks from Ground Zero.** (Danielle Richards)

Opposite left: **There was defiance. A restaurateur on Hudson Street states his case.** (Danielle Richards)

Opposite right: **The spelling is off, but the message is clear.** (Chris Pedota)

Opposite bottom: **A poster that needs no explanation.** (Carmine Galasso)

Right: **Debbie Gibaldi and several hundred others from Ridgefield, N.J., conducted a vigil for Michael Asciak, one of the first casualties to be identified. Asciak, 47, worked for Carr Futures on the 92nd floor of the North Tower. He left a wife and daughter.**
(James Anness)

Below: **The Seider family of Clifton at a candlelight vigil at City Hall. Vigils and remembrances were held all over New Jersey.**
(Norm Sutaria)

Opposite: **The view of the strangely changed skyline in the rain a few**

COMING TOGETHER

Vigils were everywhere, in small towns with a few hundred people showing up, to the bigger gatherings at Liberty State Park, to the crowd of about 30,000 at Yankee Stadium.

Amid the candles of the night watches, people touched one another in gentle, unthreatening ways — an arm on a back, a head on a shoulder, a hand grasping a hand.

Strangers wept for strangers. Some people were stoic and kept the tears inside, but you could tell from the rigidity of their jaws that they were angry, or from the quivering of those same jaws that they were grieving for people they had never met.

And never would.

Also participating in these memorials were some of the people — the kids, the mothers, the husbands, the wives — who had lost loved ones when another age of American innocence came to a crashing end. They were the ones who had had breakfast with their beloveds on Sept. 11 and then sent them to work at the World Trade Center or to the airport for a flight to the West Coast, and who would never see them again.

They were the ones whose looks of despair and disbelief and inability to understand broke your heart. You saw them and wanted to say something, but you knew you couldn't say anything meaningful.

At Yankee Stadium on Sept. 23, Catholics, Muslims, Jews, Protestants, Greek Orthodox, Sikhs, Lutherans, Presbyterians, Methodists, Hindus and, more than likely, a number of agnostics and atheists as well, filled the stands usually occupied by people yelling for El Duque, Derek, and Bernie to prevail for the Yankees.

Now, they sat fairly quietly, occasionally breaking into chants of "USA! USA!" Some waved flags. Some held up signs. Some showed pictures of friends and relatives who were missing.

Most of all, they listened. They listened to their clergy.

"Do not allow the ignorance of people to allow you to attack your good neighbors," implored Imam Izak-El M. Pasha, a New York Police Department chaplain. "We are Muslims, but we are Americans."

"We need faith, wisdom, and strength of soul," said Cardinal Edward Egan of the New York Archdiocese.

"We know who we are. They showed us who we can be," said New York Fire Department Chaplain Rabbi Joseph Potasnik of his firefighters, so many of whom were lost when the trade center collapsed.

If the people in the stands and those watching on television managed to keep a stiff upper lip during the prayer services, doubtless they succumbed to their grief when Bette Midler, singing "Wind Beneath My Wings" reached the line "Did you ever know that you're my hero," when the Harlem Boys and Girls Choir sang "We Shall Overcome" and Egan, Pasha, and Rabbi Marc Gellman joined hands and swayed, or when the tenor Placido Domingo sang "Ave Maria" in a voice as pure as the crowd's intentions.

A moment of silence at Liberty State Park during the invocation at a service for the dead and missing. Denise Gigi and Lou Gomez with candles. (Danielle Richards)

His hand on her hand, her hand on his shoulder is one way to comfort each other for Augusto and Anna Ramos of Passaic at a prayer vigil at Garret Mountain Reservation in West Paterson, N.J., (opposite). Sometimes comfort comes from just sitting close to loved ones. Staying close to Slawka Skala of Clifton, N.J., whose son, John, a Port Authority police officer, was among the missing, are her daughter, Irene Lesiw, and son-in-law, Ben Lesiw. Scott Smith, 3, and Kevin Rotolo, 4, both of Kinnelon, N.J., salute the colors as they pass.
(Beth Balbierz)

Right: **Worshiping and remembering at the New Synagogue in Fort Lee, N.J.** (Mel Evans)

Below: **Members of the North Jersey Sikh community reciting the pledge of allegiance at an interfaith service in Overpeck Park in Leonia.** (Thomas Franklin)

Opposite top: **A moment of silence at Liberty State Park during the invocation at a service for the dead and missing.** (Danielle Richards)

Opposite bottom: **Natalie Coffman, Melissa Winters, Catherine Cioffi, and Melanie Winters, all of Oradell, N.J., gather with candles at the Jersey City vigil.** (Mel Evans)

Yankee Stadium was packed
during a prayer service and
vigil 12 days after the attack
on the World Trade Center.
Steve Perna with a picture of
his best friend's wife, who was
among those killed. Elsewhere
in the grandstands were cops
with little flags coming out of
their uniform pockets, a sup-
plication to the almighty, a
woman with a picture of a
missing firefighter, and many,
many grim faces.

(Carmine Galasso)

Pallbearers, opposite page top right, with the casket of Father Mychal Judge, the New York City Fire Department chaplain who was killed by falling debris at Ground Zero while administering last rites to a fallen firefighter. Two of Judge's men, above, and a WCBS-TV cameraman, opposite page bottom, are overcome with the emotion of the day. At Holy Sepulchre Cemetery in Totowa, N.J., opposite page top left, Judge's sister receives his helmet just before he is buried.

Following page: Before attending the vigil at Liberty State Park, Daniel Pikulin walked over to the railing, took a long look at the smoke rising from the place where the World Trade Center used to be, bowed his head, and then joined the others. (Mel Evans)

Final page: The Manhattan skyline before and after the twin towers of the World Trade Center were destroyed. (AP/Mark Lennihan)

(Photo this page by Carmine Galasso, photos on opposite page, clockwise from top right by Ryan Mercer, Ryan Mercer, Kevin Wexler)